Criminal

Investigative

Policy &

Oversight

Evaluation of
Deputation of DoD Uniformed Law Enforcement
Personnel by State and Local Governments

Report Number CIPO2001S005   June 12, 2001

Office of the Inspector General
Department of Defense

Additional Copies

To obtain additional copies of this evaluation report, visit the Inspector General, DoD, home page at http://www.dodig.osd.mil/dcis/cipo/evals.htm, or contact Dr. Charles McDowell, Program Director, at (703) 604-8769 (DSN 664-8769) or Mr. John Perryman, Project Manager, at (703) 604-8765 (DSN 664-8765).

Suggestions for Future Evaluations

To suggest ideas for or to request future evaluations, contact the Audit Followup and Technical Support Directorate at (703) 604-8940 (DSN 664-8940) or fax (703) 604-8932. Ideas and requests can also be mailed to:

OAIG-AUD (ATTN: AFTS Audit Suggestions)
Inspector General, Department of Defense
400 Army Navy Drive (Room 801)
Arlington, VA 22202-4704

Defense Hotline

To report fraud, waste, or abuse, contact the Defense Hotline by calling (800) 424-9098; by sending an electronic message to Hotline@dodig.osd.mil; or by writing to the Defense Hotline, The Pentagon, Washington, D.C. 20301-1900. The identity of each writer and caller is fully protected.

Acronyms

DCIO	Defense Criminal Investigative Organization
DoD	Department of Defense
DoDD	Department of Defense Directive
DoDI	Department of Defense Instruction
IG, DoD	Inspector General, Department of Defense
USD(P&R)	Under Secretary of Defense (Personnel and Readiness)

JUN 1 2 2001

MEMORANDUM FOR UNDER SECRETARY OF DEFENSE (PERSONNEL AND READINESS)
ASSISTANT SECRETARY OF THE AIR FORCE (FINANCIAL
MANAGEMENT AND COMPTROLLER)
NAVAL INSPECTOR GENERAL
ASSISTANT SECRETARY OF THE ARMY (FINANCIAL
MANAGEMENT AND COMPTROLLER)

SUBJECT: Evaluation Report on the Deputation of DoD Uniformed Law Enforcement
Personnel by State and Local Governments (Project No. 9850023M)

We are providing this report for review and comment. Comments or suggestions from
the Navy, Air Force, and Office of the General Counsel, DoD, were considered in preparing this
report.

DoD Directive 7650.3 requires that all recommendations be resolved promptly. As a
result of management comments received, we added Recommendation 3. If management
nonconcurs with any recommendation, the comments should state the specific reasons for the
nonconcurrence and propose alternative actions, if appropriate.

We appreciate the courtesies extended to the evaluation staff. Questions on the
evaluation should be directed to Dr. Charles McDowell, Oversight Director, at (703) 604-8769
(DSN 664-8769) or Mr. John Perryman, Project Manager, at (703) 604-8765 (DSN 664-8765).
See Appendix D for the report distribution.

Charles W. Beardall
Deputy Assistant Inspector General
Criminal Investigative Policy and Oversight

Office of the Inspector General, DoD

Report No. CIPO2001S005   June 12, 2001
(Project No. 9850023M)

EVALUATION OF DEPUTATION OF DOD UNIFORMED LAW ENFORCEMENT PERSONNEL BY STATE AND LOCAL GOVERNMENTS

Executive Summary

Introduction. We announced this evaluation on June 15, 1999, and conducted our fieldwork from June 1999 through February 2000.

Objectives. Our primary objective was to determine whether DoD should issue policy governing the deputation of DoD law enforcement personnel by State and local governments. Our evaluation focused on the following sub-objectives:

- to determine the propriety of using deputized authority in view of statutory and regulatory constraints, if any;

- to determine whether the ability of DoD law enforcement organizations to perform essential law enforcement functions within their Federal jurisdiction is significantly hampered by a lack of authority to enforce State and local laws;

- to determine if the DoD law enforcement mission can be met fully and effectively with DoD assets and the assistance of State and local law enforcement agencies as necessary;

- where deputation exists, to determine if internal safeguards and management controls ensure the proper exercise of the deputized authority; and,

- to determine if the benefits that flow from DoD law enforcement agencies utilizing State or local law enforcement authority exceed the liabilities that attach to exercising such authority.

Results. We determined that neither the Office of the Secretary of Defense nor the Military Departments have issued policy to govern DoD law enforcement acquisition and use of State and local deputized police powers while on duty at DoD installations. Nevertheless, approximately 6.5 percent of military law enforcement organizations use State or local deputation to enhance their on-duty police powers.

Certain installation police officers have acquired and employed these enhanced powers without justification or sufficient oversight. Specifically, deputation has been acquired without any demonstration by the installation that the DoD law enforcement mission would be hampered without deputation. These installations have not assessed whether their DoD law enforcement mission can be met fully and effectively by employing the assistance of available State and local law enforcement resources. Local law enforcement organizations advised us that they could and would assist the DoD installations if needed. Furthermore, once obtained, many deputized powers are not used. Those deputized powers that are used are not subjected to command oversight.

Summary of Recommendations. We recommend that the Under Secretary of Defense (Personnel and Readiness) revise DoD Directive 5525.5, "DoD Cooperation with Civilian Law Enforcement Officials," January 15, 1986, to require prior approval by the Service Secretary for Service law enforcement organizations and by the Under Secretary of Defense (Personnel and Readiness) for other DoD law enforcement organizations before a DoD law enforcement organization or person may be deputized and use State or local law enforcement powers while on-duty at a DoD facility. We also recommend that the approvals conform to the guidelines set forth in Appendix C of this report. Additionally, we recommend the Military Departments establish procedures to periodically review the initial or recurrent training on the authority, scope, and extent of law enforcement authority at each installation.

Management Comments. The Air Force and Navy concurred with the report. The Army did not respond to the draft report. USD(P&R) deferred to the Office of the General Counsel, DoD. The General Counsel's office concurred with the report, suggested the additional recommendation concerning the review of recurrent training, and provided clarifying language.

Evaluation Response. We consider management comments to be fully responsive and have largely incorporated the changes suggested by the Office of the General Counsel.

EVALUATION OF DEPUTATION OF DoD UNIFORMED LAW ENFORCEMENT PERSONNEL BY STATE AND LOCAL GOVERNMENTS

TABLE OF CONTENTS

EVALUATION OF DEPUTATION OF DoD UNIFORMED LAW ENFORCEMENT PERSONNEL BY STATE AND LOCAL GOVERNMENTS

Part I - Introduction

Background

In conducting previous evaluations, we learned that some installation-level DoD law enforcement personnel advocated enhancing their Federal law enforcement authority by seeking additional authority from State or local agencies. The personnel believed that by reducing reliance on local civilian law enforcement authorities, they could enhance their ability to manage law enforcement operations on or adjacent to their installations. They cited concerns about enforcing laws involving civilian violators in areas where the Federal Government interests are only proprietary,[1] or where the Federal Government has legislative jurisdiction[2] concurrent with that of the State.[3] For example, some of their concerns were:

- without deputized authority to arrest civilians, they were uncertain of their authority to detain lawbreakers until local law enforcement officials could respond;

- without deputized authority to arrest civilians, they were uncertain about the force they could use to detain lawbreakers until local law enforcement officials arrived;

- without deputized authority to arrest civilians, they were uncertain about the extent of their personal liability exposure if they forcibly detained civilians until local law enforcement officials arrived;

---

[1] Proprietary interest is often referred to as proprietary jurisdiction. For purposes of this evaluation, we use this term to refer to a DoD location where the Federal Government has acquired some right or title to an area in a State, but has not obtained any measure of the state's authority (sovereignty) over the area. Under those circumstances, unless the State or local jurisdiction has deputized the Federal law enforcement officials, the Federal law enforcement officials may enforce Federal rules, regulations, and laws on the property, but not State or local laws and ordinances.

[2] Article I, Section 8, Clause 17, Constitution of the United States, gives States exclusive legislative jurisdiction unless a State cedes jurisdiction to the United States and the United States accepts the jurisdiction. Under the Constitution of the United States, the Congress may "... exercise exclusive Legislation in all Cases whatsoever, over such District (not exceeding ten Miles square) as may ... become the Seat of the Government of the United States, and to exercise like authority over all Places purchased by the Consent of the Legislature of the State in which the Same shall be for the Erection of Forts, Magazines, Arsenals, dock-yards and other needful buildings." In some instances, in ceding jurisdiction to the United States, a State reserved to itself the right to exercise the same powers and authorities, thereby sharing or having concurrent jurisdiction with the Federal Government.

[3] Some installation-level DoD law enforcement personnel expressed concern about their ability to enforce federal laws involving civilian violators in areas where there was concurrent jurisdiction. Their concern is the result of a misunderstanding of the law rather than a lack of actual authority, because the ability of the law enforcement official to deal with civilian violators in a concurrent jurisdiction is exactly the same as in an exclusive Federal jurisdiction.

1

- without deputized authority to arrest civilians, they were uncertain how they should respond to citizen requests for immediate police assistance while transiting through civilian communities between military facilities; and,

- they did not like the inconvenience of having to wait for a local civilian police officer to respond and take custody of a civilian offender.

The Military Departments should be able to easily address each of these concerns through recurrent training that emphasizes the authority, scope, and extent of existing installation law enforcement authority.

Civilian Law Enforcement Deputation: The Concept

State and local jurisdictions use a variety of names to identify the process for conferring law enforcement deputation. In the Commonwealth of Virginia, for example, the circuit court of any county or city may appoint "Special Conservators of the Peace" who are empowered to enforce Commonwealth laws and local ordinances. [4] In California, a Federal employee who is deputized as a "Peace Officer" may enforce state laws and ordinances. [5] Although different names are used, this process conveys state police powers upon individuals who are *not* otherwise members of a State or local law enforcement agency.

Civilian Deputation of Military Law Enforcement Officials

Section 1385 of Title 18, Unites States Code, (also known as the *Posse Comitatus* Act), prohibits the use of military personnel to enforce civilian laws, unless expressly authorized by the Constitution or an Act of Congress. The Act specifically provides that:

> "[w]hoever, except in cases and under circumstances expressly authorized by the Constitution or Act of Congress, willfully uses any part of the Army or the Air Force as a posse comitatus or otherwise to execute the laws shall be fined not more than $10,000, imprisoned not more than two years, or both." [6]

The postulated rationale behind installation-level law enforcement personnel obtaining State or local law enforcement authority to enforce State or local laws is that doing so enables personnel to deal more promptly with the civilian offenders they encounter on the installation. The authority would also allow them to provide law enforcement services in areas apart from the main installation,

---

[4] Section 19.2-13, Code of Virginia

[5] Section 830.8, California Penal Code

[6] The Act's proscriptions are made applicable to the Navy and Marine Corps by Secretary of the Navy Instruction 5820.7B, "Cooperation with Civilian Law Enforcement Officials," paragraph 9.a.(1), March 28, 1988; and DoD Directive 5525.5, "DoD Cooperation with Civilian Law Enforcement Officials," Enclosure 4, Paragraph E4.3, January 15, 1986.

including military housing that is off of the military reservation. The authority would also enable them to provide the services without having to rely on local police departments that may not be adequately staffed or deployed to deal with law enforcement issues on or adjacent to the installation. A drawback, however, is that by using State or local authority to conduct law enforcement operations, any violations of State or local law would have to be filed in local courts. Additionally, law enforcement actions would have to conform to State requirements, which may conflict with DoD policy.

Civilian Deputation in the Military Departments

We sought to identify the extent of installation-level civilian deputation within the DoD law enforcement community. Using a written survey, we contacted 92 military installations, all of which were located within the continental United States (see Appendix A). Although the responses indicated that deputation was not widely used, six Navy installations responded that they employed law enforcement personnel who had and used deputized powers in performing their Federal duties.

Objectives, Scope, and Methodology

Our primary objective was to determine whether DoD should issue policy governing the deputation of DoD law enforcement personnel by State and local governments. Our evaluation focused on the following sub-objectives:[7]

- to determine the propriety of using deputized authority in view of statutory and regulatory constraints, if any;

- to determine whether the ability of DoD law enforcement organizations to perform essential law enforcement functions within their Federal jurisdiction is significantly impaired by a lack of authority to enforce State and local laws;

- to determine if the DoD law enforcement mission can be met fully and effectively with the assistance of State and local law enforcement agencies as needed;[8]

- where deputation exists, to determine if internal safeguards and management controls ensure the proper exercise of the deputized authority; and,

---

[7] Objectives were derived from U.S. Attorney General Memorandum, "Guidelines for Legislation Involving Federal Criminal Law Enforcement Authority," June 29, 1984. At the time of this evaluation, we validated that the guidelines were current and that changes were not anticipated.

[8] More specifically, we wanted to know whether there is an adverse impact on DoD law enforcement officers' mission if they must continue to rely on State and local law enforcement organizations to address non-Federal crimes that civilians commit on or near military installations.

- to determine if the benefits that flow from DoD law enforcement agencies using State or local law enforcement authority exceed the liabilities that attach to exercising such authority.

We visited the locations identified through our survey as having deputized law enforcement personnel. We also visited comparable military installations in the same states that did *not* use deputized powers, although they would face similar law enforcement challenges. At both types of locations, we interviewed Service legal representatives; law enforcement policy proponents; field law enforcement supervisory and operations personnel (both military and civil service); and local civilian law enforcement and legal representatives, including those responsible for granting deputation. We also coordinated certain legal aspects of this evaluation with the Office of General Counsel, DoD, and the Criminal and Civil Divisions, Department of Justice.

The scope of our evaluation did not include examining the use of deputized powers by off-duty DoD military or civilian law enforcement personnel for non-Federal purposes, or the use of deputized authority by part-time DoD employees or volunteers. Further, our evaluation focused on installation police department type organizations. However, our findings would apply to other DoD police organizations, including those employed at the Pentagon and Defense agencies.

We performed our fieldwork between June 1999 and February 2000.

EVALUATION OF DEPUTATION OF DoD UNIFORMED LAW ENFORCEMENT PERSONNEL BY STATE AND LOCAL GOVERNMENTS

Part II- Evaluation Results and Recommendations

Need For DoD Policy and Process

The DoD law enforcement community does not have a process for determining the appropriateness of using deputized law enforcement powers. The condition exists because DoD does not have specific policy that addresses the issue. As a result, law enforcement decisions regarding deputation are being made at the installation level, and a clear risk exists that military law enforcement organizations may extend their enforcement powers beyond legal authority with neither a demonstrated need nor effective oversight.

Introduction

We visited the bases that told us they had police officers who used deputized powers while on duty. We wanted to know whether those police officers, when performing DoD functions, relied on deputized powers to carry firearms; execute search or arrest warrants; make warrantless arrests; and serve legal processes, administer oaths or affirmations; or use covert investigative techniques.[9] For comparison purposes, we also visited military installations that told us they did not use deputized powers. Details of our findings at some of the installations are set forth in Appendix B.

Overall, we visited 6 military installations that either used or intended to use deputation, and 11 that did not. Supervisors at one base that reported using deputation briefed us on their deputized powers. We ultimately learned, however, that the base did not have officers who actually were deputized.[10] At another base, which we visited for comparison purposes, we learned that the law enforcement personnel had been deputized by one local jurisdiction and were pursuing deputation from other jurisdictions.[11]

---

[9] We characterized covert investigative techniques as those generally recognized and utilized for covert operations, including electronic surveillance, undercover operations, and paid informants.

[10] This misinformation demonstrated the lack of an effective oversight process for deputation that had led managers and officers to assume they had powers they did not have.

[11] Police officers at this base had not begun using their deputized powers, but intended to do so.

Are There Statutory and Regulatory Constraints?

To determine the propriety of using deputized authority in view of statutory and regulatory constraints, we initially researched the legal authority for deputation. We found that no law or regulation expressly authorizes or prohibits deputation; the legal authority for deputation lies in the inherent authority of commanders to provide for the safety and security of their installations. That legal authority places significant constraints on the functions of authorizing and exercising deputation.

Constraints on Authorizing Deputation. The decision to obtain deputation authority from State or local civilian authorities must be made by the installation commander. The commander's decision must be based on the commander's determination that obtaining deputation authority is necessary to ensure the safety and security of the installation or to accomplish some other military purpose inherent in the commander's mission. The determination must be based upon a comprehensive review of the particular facts at that installation, including factors addressed in the following four sections of this report and must be a reasonable and rational exercise of the commander's discretion.

Constraints on Executing Deputation Authority. Installation law enforcement personnel receive deputation authority solely to accomplish the law enforcement function for that installation as defined by the installation commander. They may, therefore, use the deputation authority only in furtherance of the defined law enforcement function. The constraint should be a significant issue when discussing acquisition of deputation authority with State and local authorities. State and local authorities must understand the limits that the installation commander places on exercising the deputation authority. They must also accept that, if any conflict between a State or local requirement exists for exercising deputation and the installation commander's law enforcement requirements, installation law enforcement personnel must always comply with their commander's requirements. Any exercise of deputation authority beyond the limit set by the installation commander may subject installation law enforcement personnel to personal liability and may violate the *Posse Comitatus* Act (see below for additional information regarding this Act).

We were unable to identify the DoD policy that specifically addresses the issue of local law enforcement deputation for DoD personnel to assist in performing their DoD mission. In addition, the Services do not have written guidance on using deputized powers, either at the Service headquarters or installation level.

Only DoD Directive 5525.5, "DoD Cooperation with Civilian Law Enforcement Officials," January 15, 1986, provides peripherally relevant guidance. The directive establishes DoD policy on cooperating with civilian law enforcement and provides:

"It is DoD policy to cooperate with civilian law enforcement officials to the extent practical. The implementation of this policy shall be consistent with the needs of national security and military preparedness, the historic tradition of limiting direct military involvement in civilian law enforcement activities, and the requirements of applicable law, as developed in enclosures E2. through E7."

Enclosure E4. of the Directive, "Restrictions on Participation of DoD Personnel in Civilian Law Enforcement Activities," permits certain specified direct assistance to civilian law enforcement, including:

"E4.1.2.1. Actions that are taken for the primary purpose of furthering a military or foreign affairs function of the United States, regardless of incidental benefits to civilian authorities."

One type of direct assistance permissible under this provision, depending on the nature of the DoD interest and the authority governing the specific action, is:

"E4.1.2.1.3. Investigations and other actions related to the commander's inherent authority to maintain law and order on a military installation or facility."

The policy, however, specifically cautions against "… actions taken for the primary purpose of aiding civilian law enforcement officials or otherwise serving as a subterfuge to avoid the restrictions of [the *Posse Comitatus* Act]."[12] The caution would not appear to be relevant to the Federal uses of State and local deputation under review in this evaluation. The Act (18 U.S.C. §1385) generally prohibits the use of the military to enforce civilian laws, but a recognized exception to the general rule, memorialized in DoD regulations, is the inherent authority of a military commander to maintain law and order on the military installation or at a military facility. The uses of deputized power we examined were presumably sought and used for the purpose of enhancing the installation commander's ability to safeguard the military community and its personnel. [13]

In summary, 18 U.S.C. §1385 generally prohibits the use of the military to enforce civilian laws, but a recognized exception to the general rule, memorialized in DoD regulations, is the inherent authority of a military commander to maintain law and order on a military installation or at a military facility

---

[12] Paragraph E4.1.2.1., DoD Directive 5525.5, "DoD Cooperation with Civilian Law Enforcement Officials," January 15, 1986.

[13] This is not to say, however, that the use of those powers could not potentially result in a violation of the Act if, for example, the powers are exercised beyond the needs of the military installation. We note also that even if the military installation law enforcement officers involved are civilian employees, they are not exempted by DoD Directive 5525.5 from the provision of the *Posse Comitatus* Act when under the command and control of a military officer such as an installation commander.

Is Mission Accomplishment Impaired?

None of the installations we visited needed deputized powers to authorize personnel to carry firearms, serve legal process, administer oaths or affirmations, or use covert investigative techniques while performing their official police duties. The officers either already possessed sufficient authority for those purposes, or the nature of their duties did not require additional authority.

We then sought to determine whether the officers needed deputized powers to execute arrest and search warrants or to make warrantless arrests, and whether their mission accomplishment would be significantly diminished without those deputized powers. Overall, we found that installations with officers possessing those deputized powers did not need the additional powers to meet their law enforcement responsibilities. Some officers *preferred* to have deputized powers, principally because doing so enabled them to write State traffic violation notices. Police managers at three of the installations stated that, based on their experience, State traffic violation notices are more effective than the DD 1805, "United States District Court Violations Notice," and DD 1408, "Armed Forces Traffic Ticket." According to the personnel, depending on the State involved, form DD 1805 and 1408 violations were either not posted to State driver license records consistently, or the postings were not permitted at all (Appendix B). Another officer used his deputation to file charges with the local prosecutor, who reportedly preferred to receive charges filed by a State-deputized officer. That officer asserted that the installation relied on the local prosecutor because the servicing Federal magistrate did not want to adjudge the base's minor cases; the U.S. Attorney's Office that serviced the installation denied the assertion.

Is State and Local Assistance Effective?

Using State or local deputation to enhance DoD law enforcement authority could be prudent at installations where local civilian law enforcement agencies with primary police authority are unable to address civilian crimes impacting Government property or personnel. To determine whether the DoD law enforcement mission could be met effectively without such deputation, we visited the principal civilian law enforcement agencies at three of the five locations where deputized powers were being used. Those civilian law enforcement agencies advised us that higher priority, exigent circumstances outside the installation might occasionally impact response time to the installation. However, none said that they could not or would not support DoD law enforcement personnel. In addition, none of the installations we visited had validated that local law enforcement was incapable of providing the necessary support before they sought deputation.

Are Management Controls Adequate?

To determine if adequate internal safeguards and management controls are in place to ensure the proper exercise of State-deputized authority, we asked Service headquarters police management offices for their policies that specifically addressed the use of deputized powers. None of the offices had such policies. Therefore, they did not have inspection processes that directly addressed oversight needs for the use of deputized powers.

At the six locations that used or intended to use deputized powers, we asked if they had local written policy or operating instructions governing the use of deputized powers. Only one location had developed written policy covering training for and exercise of such powers. At another location, a Service legal opinion held that extant police authorities, without deputation, were sufficient for security personnel to fully discharge responsibilities. The same legal opinion, after noting that Federal law or regulation did not prohibit deputation, recommended limits on the authority and that permissible deputized actions be clearly detailed in written command guidelines. They were not.

In summary, the Services do not have policy addressing use of deputized powers, and most locations with deputized powers do not have operating instructions or other written guidance regulating the use of those powers.

Do Benefits Outweigh Liabilities?

We could not determine if the benefits from DoD law enforcement agencies using State or local deputation exceeded the potential liabilities. None of the locations with deputized powers was required to articulate such a determination in requesting deputation. At each location with deputized powers, the local civilian authorities concurred in the DoD law enforcement personnel exercising deputized powers but without persuasive justification that deputation was needed for public order. Of course, deputation would reduce demand for services placed against the local civilian law enforcement agency, but this result is not in and of itself a benefit for DoD law enforcement.

On the issue of liability, our review did not identify instances where civil or criminal court actions were initiated against DoD uniformed police officers because they exercised deputized powers. Nevertheless, expansions in police powers and its application to a larger populace increases the potential for liability.

Conclusion

We determined that neither the Office of the Secretary of Defense nor the Military Departments have issued policy to govern DoD law enforcement acquisition and of State and local deputized police powers while on duty at DoD installations.

Deputation has been acquired without demonstrating that the lack of deputation would significantly hamper the DoD law enforcement mission. Additionally, where deputation exists, it has not been shown that local law enforcement agencies would not provide adequate law enforcement assistance if requested. Once obtained, many deputized powers are not used, even though they are not constrained by command directives, which suggests the additional powers are not needed. Further, deputized powers that are exercised while on-duty are not subjected to command directives. While the deputation probably reduced DoD demand for police services placed against the local law enforcement agency, that result was not in and of itself a benefit for DoD law enforcement and would not outweigh potential increases in liability.

Recommendations, Management Comments and Evaluation Response

1. We recommend that the Under Secretary of Defense (Personnel and Readiness) revise DoD Directive 5525.5, "DoD Cooperation with Civilian Law Enforcement Officials," January 15, 1986, to require prior approval by the Service Secretary or designee for Service law enforcement organizations and by the Under Secretary of Defense (Personnel and Readiness) or designee for other DoD law enforcement organizations before a DoD law enforcement organization or person may use deputized State or local law enforcement powers while on duty at a DoD facility.

2. We recommend that approvals for a DoD law enforcement organization or person to use deputized State or local law enforcement powers while on duty conform to the guidelines set forth in Appendix C of this report.

3. We recommend the Military Departments establish procedures to periodically review the initial or recurrent training on the authority, scope, and extent of law enforcement authority at each installation.

Management Comments

The Air Force and Navy concurred with the report. The Army did not respond to the draft report. USD(P&R) deferred to the Office of the General Counsel, DoD. The General Counsel's office concurred with the report, suggested the addition of the third recommendation, and provided suggestions for clarifying language.

Evaluation Response

We consider management comments to be fully responsive and have largely incorporated the suggested changes by the Office of the General Counsel.

Appendix A. Survey of Military Service Law Enforcement Organizations to Identify Those with Deputized State or Local Police Powers

METHODOLOGY

We identified all Army, Navy, Air Force, and Marine Corps installations with a total population (active duty and civil service) greater than 500. A total of 243 installations (78 Army, 76 Navy, 72 Air Force, and 17 Marine Corps) were identified.

After coordinating with the Quantitative Methods Division, Office of the Assistant Inspector General for Auditing, we determined that approximately 90 installations would constitute a representative sample. We then calculated the percentage that each Service represented in the 243 installations and applied them to the randomly selected sample (N=90), rounding up as the percentage calculations warranted. The result was a 92 installation actual sample, consisting of 30 Army, 28 Navy, 28 Air Force, and 6 Marine Corps installations.

We then sorted the total population (243 installations) by Service and population, from largest to smallest, and identified the median population. We regarded those bases with populations above the median as large installations, and those with populations below the median as small installations. After assigning index numbers to each base, we randomly selected an equal number of large and small installation for each Service until we reached that Service's share of the 92 installations sample size. Survey questionnaires were then sent to the 92 installations.

RESULTS OF SURVEY

The response rate for our written survey was 100 percent. In responding to the survey, six installations (all Navy bases), or 6.5 percent of the total, reported that their law enforcement personnel used deputized police powers.[14] The bases reported the following reasons for deputation.

---

[14] During our field visits, we determined that Base 2 did not have or use deputized police powers.

Table 1
Reasons Given For Using Deputation

Base*	Additional Local Police Training	To File Charges In Local Courts	Portion of Work In Proprietary Jurisdiction	Portion of Work in Concurrent Jurisdiction	Insufficient Commanding Officer Authority	Other
1		X	X	X		
2			X			X
3		X	X		X	
4	X	X	X	X		
5		X		X		
6		X	X			
Total	1	5	5	3	1	1

* Base 1 is Norfolk Naval Base, Virginia; Base 2 is Naval Air Station North Island, California; Base 3 is Naval Air Weapons Station China Lake, California ; Base 4 is Naval Weapons Station Charleston, South Carolina; Base 5 is Naval Air Station Brunswick, Maine; and Base 6 is Naval Weapons Station Yorktown, Virginia.

Types of Deputized Personnel

- Three of the six law enforcement organizations permitted both military and civil service law enforcement officers to exercise deputized powers while on duty.

- Three of the six law enforcement organizations permitted only civil service law enforcement officers to exercise deputized powers.

- None of the six organizations permitted contract security officers to exercise deputized powers while on duty.

Management Oversight

Table 2
Types of Personnel Deputized and
Types of Management Oversight Exercised

Base	Deputized Personnel	Written Guidance On Using Deputized Powers	Initial Deputation Training Required	Recurring Deputation Training Required
1	Military and Civil Service	Yes	No	No
2*	Military and Civil Service	Yes	Yes	Yes
3	Military and Civil Service	Yes	Yes	No
4	Civil Service	No	Yes	Yes
5	Civil Service	Yes	Yes	No
6	Civil Service	No	Yes	No

* As previously noted, during field visits we determined that Base 2 did not have or use deputized powers.

- According to the survey responses, two of the six law enforcement organizations did not have written guidance governing how and when deputized powers can be used while performing official U.S. Government duties. Those results are at variance with our on-site evaluation work. We found that only one location, Base 4, had written guidance covering the use of deputized powers.

Appendix B. **How Bases Use Deputized Powers**

BASE 1, BASE 3, AND BASE 4

Three bases had more than one police officer with State or local government deputation used to enforce state law while on Federal duty. Police managers at all three locations advised that using deputized powers to request and execute arrest or search warrants was extremely rare. The police managers indicated that although they used deputized powers to make warrantless arrests, the powers were primarily used to issue misdemeanor summonses or traffic violation notices. Two of the bases were predominately concurrent jurisdictions, and one was predominantly proprietary jurisdiction.

Personnel at both bases with concurrent jurisdiction (Bases 1 and 4) maintained that their authorities to issue DD 1805, "United States District Court Violation Notice", and DD 1408, "Armed Forces Traffic Ticket," were not a sufficient deterrent to violators. The personnel claimed that the *Armed Forces Traffic Ticket* adjudicated in a base administrative process could not be posted to the violator's State driving record. Similarly, personnel claimed that the *United States District Court Violation Notice* lacked a consistent process for notifying the violator's state driver's licensing agency.[15] Further, personnel at both locations claimed that the servicing Federal District Court did not want their traffic and misdemeanor cases.

We attempted to validate the claim that the Federal District Court did not want to hear traffic and misdemeanor cases from the base. At one location, the United States Attorney's Office reviewed, with the responsible Federal Magistrate, the obligation to hear all cases under Federal jurisdiction. The United States Attorney's Office then reported to us that any Federal Magistrate's reluctance to hear the cases would not be a continuing concern. With respect to the other base with concurrent Federal and State jurisdiction, representatives from the servicing United States Attorney's Office told us they knew they could not limit military access to Federal courts, and Federal Magistrates in the district would not decline to hear any case within their jurisdiction. However, they thought that presenting traffic violations and misdemeanor crimes in state courts would be a more efficient use of Federal court and prosecutor resources.

---

[15] The Central Violations Bureau, which manages or monitors the *United States District Court Violations Notices,* told us that they have agreements with some states to post such traffic violations to violator driving records. If the person sends in the fine, which they refer to as a "collateral forfeiture," the Bureau forwards a notice to the violator's state licensing agency, assuming they have an agreement with the agency. If the person takes his or her chance in court and is convicted by the Federal Magistrate, it is up to the court to notify the violator's state licensing agency. The Bureau doubted that the Federal Magistrates notify the States very often.

At Base 3, which had predominately proprietary jurisdiction, police managers pointed out that proprietary jurisdiction presented certain law enforcement challenges. The managers observed that Federal courts do not have jurisdiction over most traffic violations, misdemeanor crimes, or felony crimes that occur on base and, therefore, they cannot use DD 1805, "United States District Court Violation Notice." Similarly, they asserted that DD 1408, "Armed Forces Traffic Ticket," is not an effective deterrent for traffic violators because the on-base administrative adjudication process is not sufficient to allow violations to be posted to the violator's state driving record.[16] In addition, according to the police managers, their law enforcement efforts are also impeded because State law normally only permits arrests for misdemeanor crimes if the police officer personally witnesses the crime. They asserted that civil service and military police officers at the base do not have arrest authority and can only detain a civilian for civil authorities. When they call the local police for misdemeanor crimes, the military and civil service policeman who witnessed the crime must sign the complaint stating that they have made a citizen's arrest.[17] At that point, the local police officer can take custody of the person because the officer is merely accepting custody of an arrestee.[18] The police managers believe that relying on citizen arrest authority increases the officer's civil liability, and because it is conduct that occurs while on duty, the Government's liability is also increased.[19]

BASE 5 AND BASE 6

Two bases had one officer with deputized powers. Both locations were predominately concurrent jurisdiction facilities. Both locations previously had several more deputized personnel, but as the personnel retired or transferred, their replacements were not deputized. The use of deputized officers at Base 6 will end when the remaining officer retires. At that location, the officer uses his deputized authority to write State uniform summonses for traffic violations in a proprietary

---

[16] The State's Department of Motor Vehicles verified the assertion. The State code allows only "convictions" to be posted to the driver's record, and the results of administrative processes are not considered "convictions."

[17] A citizen's arrest is defined by Merriam-Webster Dictionary as an arrest made not by a law officer but by a citizen who derives authority from the fact of being a citizen.

[18] While visiting comparison sites where deputized powers were not used while on duty, we found that citizen's arrests were used at one Navy and two Air Force bases.

[19] The Office of Enforcement Operations, Criminal Division, United States Department of Justice, has a similar opinion. Personnel at this office explained that citizen arrest authority could differ state-to-state. Some states include this authority in statute. Other states rely on common law principles. The authorities or responsibilities of the person making a citizen's arrest can be murky, and there can be considerable room for interpretation by a local magistrate. The application of citizen's arrest in a particular jurisdiction may require a retreat until no longer practical or something similar, and retreating is not a typical practice for a law enforcement officer. They also cited the fact that a citizen who makes an arrest must be right, i.e., the person they arrest must have committed the crime. On rare occasions, reasonable belief or some similar police officer standard may be permitted for an ordinary citizen (a person without statutory authority) who denies another's freedom to move. The use of force to make a citizen's arrest for a misdemeanor may *not* be permitted in some or most states. They thought reliance on citizen's arrest powers could make resisting arrest a very challenging standard to apply. Further, variance in state laws could confuse the issues from one jurisdiction to the next.

housing area. The officer writes 7 to 10 traffic violations per week. When the deputized officer is not on duty, the other police officers simply warn traffic violators. The one deputized officer does not make arrests because, if he did, the military base would be required to pay the confinement fees at the local jail. Serious infractions by civilians are turned over to local civilian police who directly incur the confinement costs. Infractions by military personnel are referred to their chain of command. The deputized officer does not execute arrest or search warrants.

At Base 5, the one deputized officer is a Navy police detective. The location is predominantly concurrent jurisdiction, and the traffic citation issued is DD 1408, "Armed Forces Traffic Ticket." The traffic tickets are adjudicated on base under an administrative process. More serious complaints, such as driving under the influence, are sent to the Navy detective who is also a "Special Police Officer" for the State.[20] The detective told us that he files the paper work with the District Attorney's Office because that office prefers receiving it from a State-certified police officer. The detective explained that the initial decision to seek deputized police powers was made because the servicing Federal District Court did not want to handle minor cases. Although the detective also has authority to request and serve search warrants, the last time he did so was in 1992, during an investigation into the theft of Government property.

Our contacts did not validate the assertions concerning the Federal District Court. We contacted the Supervisor, Criminal Division, U.S. Attorney's Office, and were told that Federal Magistrates in the state process all violations cited on the DD 1805 form. The supervisor advised us that she had never heard of a policy that discourages presentation of misdemeanor cases in the Federal District Court.

COMPARISON BASE WITH DEPUTIZED POWERS

While visiting one comparison site, an Air Force base, we learned that police officers at the base had received deputation from one local jurisdiction, though it was not yet being exercised while on duty, and the base was negotiating additional deputation with other local jurisdictions. The Air Force base was in an urban area and had law enforcement services that extended to six venues, all with only Federal proprietary jurisdiction. For the six areas combined, the base relies on assistance from local law enforcement approximately 50 times a year. During 1999, base police officers issued 131 moving traffic summons, including 4 for driving under the influence, using DD 1408, "Armed Forces Traffic Ticket."

---

[20] State of Maine Statutes Title 30-A, §2671.

Appendix C. Guidelines for Approving Use of Deputized State or Local Law Enforcement Powers by DoD Uniformed Law Enforcement Personnel While On Duty[21]

1. GENERAL

Organizations performing DoD missions should *not* expand their law enforcement authorities by seeking deputized State or local law enforcement authority unless:

a. ability to perform an essential command law enforcement function within the jurisdiction is significantly hampered by a lack of authority to enforce State or local laws;

b. need for such law enforcement authority cannot be met effectively by assistance from law enforcement agencies with such authority;

c. adequate internal safeguards and management controls exist to ensure proper exercise of the authority;

d. advantages to possessing the authority can reasonably be expected to exceed the disadvantages likely involved in exercising the authority; and

e. authority to use deputation from State or local government has been approved by the Under Secretary of Defense (Personnel and Readiness) or the Secretary of a Military Department or designee.

2. REQUESTS AND APPROVAL AUTHORITY

a. For requests that justify the need and otherwise comply with the guidelines contained herein, the Under Secretary of Defense (Personnel and Readiness), the Secretary of a Military Department, or designee should approve requests for DoD civilian or military law enforcement personnel (hereafter referred to in aggregate as DoD law enforcement personnel, or DoD employees) to use, while on Government duty, deputized powers from State or local government.

---

[21] Guidelines were adapted from Attorney General Memorandum, "Guidelines for Legislation Involving Federal Criminal Law Enforcement Authority," June 29, 1984.

b. For DoD law enforcement personnel to use deputized State or local law enforcement authority while performing DoD functions, military commanders and law enforcement organization managers should request, through their chains-of-command, approval for DoD law enforcement personnel to use State or local law enforcement authority while performing DoD functions. The DoD law enforcement personnel must present written justification in support of the request, and the justification should comply with the following guidelines, as applicable. The written justification should provide all relevant information including: (1) a detailed discussion of the issues identified in paragraphs 1a-d above, (2) the concurrence or non-concurrence, and any comments, of the appropriate U.S. Attorney who would handle legal actions arising from the exercise of the deputation authority , and (3) a written statement from the State or local official issuing the deputation authorization agreeing with the scope of the delegation authority as defined by the installation commander and acknowledging that deputized installation law enforcement personnel will not comply with any State or local requirements that conflict in any way with federal law or the installation commander's requirements.

3. GUIDELINES

a. **Authority to Carry a Firearm.** DoD law enforcement personnel should *not* rely on deputized State or local law enforcement authority to carry a firearm while on duty unless:

(1) there is a significant likelihood that, in the course of performing assigned duties, the DoD employee will be placed in situations where use of a firearm would be legally permissible only if deputized by State or local authorities to:

(i) protect himself/herself from a threat of imminent death, serious bodily injury, or kidnapping;

(ii) prevent another person from causing imminent death or bodily injury to, or kidnapping of, a person who is under his/her protection; or

(iii) prevent the imminent loss or destruction of, or damage to, property of substantial value that is under his/her protection;

(2) it is unlikely that timely and effective assistance would be available from another agency with requisite police powers;

(3) the DoD employee has graduated from an accredited training course in using the particular deputized State or local authority to carry and use firearms, and is currently qualified in the use; and

(4) the requestor agrees that, should the use of deputized authority be granted, policies and procedures will be established and implemented to prevent the

unauthorized use or misuse of firearms by the DoD employees covered in the request. Policies and procedures must include a requirement for a designated senior official to specifically authorize each DoD employee covered in the request to carry a firearm under the deputized authority.

b. **Authority to Seek and Execute an Arrest or Search Warrant.** A DoD employee should not seek or execute an arrest warrant or search warrant under deputized State or local law enforcement authority, unless there is reason to believe the person to whom the authority would be applied has committed an offense within DoD law enforcement jurisdiction, or the person committed an offense involving resistance to the DoD employee's law enforcement authority, or the authority is necessary to search for and seizure property related to such offenses, and:

(1) a significant likelihood exists that in the course of performing assigned duties, the DoD employee will frequently encounter situations in which it is necessary to rely on deputized State or local law enforcement powers to obtain needed arrest or search warrants;

(2) it is unlikely that timely and effective assistance would be available from another agency;

(3) the DoD employee has graduated from an accredited training course in executing arrest and search warrants based on the particular deputized State or local law enforcement authority; and

(4) the requestor agrees that, should deputized authority be granted, policies and procedures will be established and implemented to prevent unauthorized DoD employee use or misuse of deputized State or local law enforcement authority to obtain and execute arrest or search warrants.

c. **Authority to Make a Warrantless Arrest.** DoD employees should not make an arrest without a warrant using deputized State or local law enforcement authority unless the DoD employee has probable cause to believe the person being arrested has committed a felony, or commits a felony or misdemeanor crime in the DoD employee's presence; and

(1) a significant likelihood exists that, in the course of performing assigned duties, the DoD employee will frequently encounter situations in which it is necessary to rely on deputized State or local law enforcement powers to make an arrest promptly;

(2) it is unlikely that timely and effective assistance will be available from another agency;

(3) the DoD employee has graduated from an accredited training course in making arrests based on the particular deputized State or local law enforcement authority; and

(4) the requestor agrees that, should deputized authority be granted, policies and procedures will be established and implemented to prevent unauthorized DoD employee use or misuse of the deputized State and local law enforcement authority to make arrests.

d. **Authority to Serve a Grand Jury Subpoena or Other Legal Process.** A DoD employee should *not* rely on State or local deputized law enforcement authority to serve a grand jury subpoena, a summons, a court order, or other legal process, unless:

(1) a significant likelihood exists that, in the course of performing assigned duties, the DoD employee will frequently encounter situations in which it is necessary to rely on deputized State or local law enforcement authority to serve such process;

(2) it is unlikely that other agency personnel could service the process on a timely basis;

(3) the DoD employee has been trained in the serving process based on the particular deputized State or local law enforcement authority; and

(4) the requestor agrees that, should deputized authority be granted, policies and procedures will be established and implemented to prevent unauthorized DoD employee use or misuse of the deputized State or local law enforcement authority to serve process.

e. **Authority to Administer an Oath or Affirmation.** A DoD employee should *not* rely on State or local deputized law enforcement authority to administer an oath or affirmation, unless:

(1) a significant likelihood exists that, in the course of performing assigned duties, the DoD employee will frequently encounter situations in which it is necessary or desirable to rely on State or local law enforcement authority to administer an oath or affirmation and take a person's statement or testimony under oath or affirmation;

(2) it is unlikely that other agency personnel could administer the oath or affirmation conveniently and expeditiously;

(3) the DoD employee has been trained in administering oaths and affirmations based on the particular deputized State or local law enforcement authority; and

(4) the requestor agrees that, should deputized authority be granted, policies and procedures will be established and implemented to prevent unauthorized DoD employees use or misuse of the deputized State or local law enforcement authority to administer oaths or affirmations.

f. **Authority to Use a Covert Investigative Technique.** A DoD employee should *not* rely on State or local deputized law enforcement authority to use a covert investigative technique, unless:

(1) a significant likelihood exists that, in the course of performing assigned duties, the DoD employee will frequently encounter situations in which it is necessary to rely on deputized State or local law enforcement authority to use such a covert investigative technique;

(2) it is unlikely that timely and effective assistance from an agency with expertise in using the covert investigative technique will be available;

(3) the DoD employee has graduated from an accredited training course in using the covert investigative technique based on the deputized State or local authority; and

(4) the requestor agrees that, should deputized authority be granted, policies and procedures will be established and implemented to prevent unauthorized DoD employees use or misuse, or the appearance thereof, of the covert investigative technique. The policies and procedures should include the requirement for a designated senior official to approve the DoD employee's use of a covert investigative technique based on deputized State or local government authority.

Appendix D. **Report Distribution**

Office of the Secretary of Defense

Under Secretary of Defense (Personnel and Readiness)*
Assistant Secretary of Defense (Command, Control, Communications and Intelligence)*
General Counsel, Department of Defense*

Department of the Army

Assistant Secretary of the Army (Financial Management and Comptroller)*
Assistant Secretary of the Army (Manpower and Reserve Affairs)*
General Counsel, Department of the Army*
Inspector General, Department of the Army*
Auditor General, Department of the Army*
Deputy Chief of Staff for Operations and Plans*
Commander, U.S. Army Criminal Investigation Command*

Department of the Navy

Assistant Secretary of the Navy (Manpower & Reserve Affairs)*
General Counsel, Department of the Navy*
Inspector General, Department of the Navy*
Director, Naval Criminal Investigative Service*
Deputy Commandant, Plans, Policies and Operations, Headquarters, U.S. Marine Corps*
Inspector General, U.S. Marine Corps*

Department of the Air Force

Assistant Secretary of the Air Force (Financial Management & Comptroller)*
General Counsel, Department of the Air Force*
Inspector General, Department of the Air Force*
Commander, Air Force Office of Special Investigations*
Director of Security Forces*

Other Defense Organizations

General Counsel, Defense Logistics Agency
Inspector General, National Security Agency
Inspector General, Defense Intelligence Agency

Non-Defense Federal Organizations

None

Congressional Committees and Subcommittees, Chairman and Ranking Minority Member

Senate Committee on Appropriations
Senate Subcommittee on Defense, Committee on Appropriations
Senate Committee on Armed Services
Senate Committee on Governmental Affairs
House Committee on Appropriations
House Subcommittee on Defense, Committee on Appropriations
House Committee on Armed Services
House Committee on Government Reform
House Subcommittee on Government Efficiency, Financial Management, and
    Intergovernmental Relations, Committee on Government Reform
House Subcommittee on National Security, Veterans Affairs, and International Relations,
    Committee on Government Reform

*Recipient of draft report.

DEPARTMENT OF THE NAVY

HEADQUARTERS
NAVAL CRIMINAL INVESTIGATIVE SERVICE
WASHINGTON NAVY YARD BLDG 111
716 SICARD STREET SE
WASHINGTON DC 20388-5380

27 Oct 2000

MEMORANDUM FOR DEPARTMENT OF DEFENSE INSPECTOR GENERAL
(CRIMINAL INVESTIGATIVE POLICY AND OVERSIGHT)

Subj: EVALUATION OF DEPUTATION OF DOD UNIFORMED LAW
        ENFORCEMENT PERSONNEL BY STATE AND LOCAL GOVERNMENT
        (PROJECT NUMBER 9850023M)

Ref: (a) DODIG Memorandum dtd Sep 7, 2000

In response to reference (a), the cited draft report was
reviewed by the Naval Criminal Investigative Service (NCIS)
for comments/recommendations as appropriate.

NCIS concurs with the recommendations as indicated in the
report and submits no further comments.

If additional information and/or assistance is needed,
please do not hesitate to contact Ms. Joyce Morris, NCIS
Office of Inspections at (202)433-9598.

VERONICA MCCARTHY
Assistant Director
  for Inspections

Copy to:
File

DEPARTMENT OF THE AIR FORCE
HEADQUARTERS UNITED STATES AIR FORCE
WASHINGTON, DC

3 0 OCT 2000

MEMORANDUM FOR DEPUTY ASSISTANT INSPECTOR GENERAL INVESTIGATIVE
POLICY AND OVERSIGHT OFFICE OF THE INSPECTOR
GENERAL DEPARTMENT OF DEFENSE

FROM: AF/XOF

SUBJECT: DoDIG Draft Report, Evaluation of Deputation of DoD Uniformed Law
Enforcement Personnel by State and Local Government (Project Code 98550023M)

The Air Force concurs with the report as written. There is no existing need for blanket
deputation of security forces personnel. The recommendation to require prior approval from the
appropriate Service Secretary and the Under Secretary of Defense for Personnel and Readiness
or his/her designee before an organization or person may use deputized state or local power
while on duty is appropriate and provides an avenue if the need should arise.

HQ USAF/XO POC is SMSgt O'Connor. If you have any questions, he can be reached
at (703) 588-0025.

MARTIN D. GIERE, Col, USAF
Deputy Director of Security Forces

DEPARTMENT OF DEFENSE
OFFICE OF GENERAL COUNSEL
1600 DEFENSE PENTAGON
WASHINGTON, DC 20301-1600

23 May 2001

MEMORANDUM FOR INSPECTOR GENERAL OF THE DEPARTMENT OF DEFENSE
(Attn: Mr. John Perryman)

SUBJECT: Draft Report on the Evaluation of Deputation of DoD Uniformed Law Enforcement
Personnel by State and Local Governments (Project No. 9850023M)

Thank you for the opportunity to provide additional comments regarding this well-researched
and well-crafted draft report. I have completed my legal review and incorporate my conclusions
in my comments which key to the applicable section of the draft report.

Executive Summary. The draft report lists five objectives. The fifth objective is "to determine
the propriety of using deputized authority in view of statutory and regulatory constraints, if any."
This objective may be better placed as the first objective because all subsequent analysis,
encompassed in the other objectives, flows from and must comply with these legal constraints.
The draft report actually recognizes the primacy of this objective by addressing it before the
other four in Part II, Introduction. This comment also applies to the list of the objectives on page
3, Background.

Table of Contents. Under Part II, adding a new section after the "Introduction" section would
enhance the structure and flow of the draft report. The new section might be named "Statutory
and Regulatory Constraints" and would address the fifth objective. As currently drafted, the
"Introduction" section's first six paragraphs address the fifth objective while only the last two
paragraphs provide introductory information. The "Introduction" paragraph might better include
only those last two paragraphs. The new "Statutory and Regulatory Constraints" section would
include the first six paragraphs (and some additional paragraphs I suggest below). The reason
for this recommendation is to address clearly the legal constraints issues in a separate section that
would set the stage for the remaining analysis.

Part I, footnote 3, last line. The word "current" might be a typo for "concurrent." In addition,
since this discussion apparently relates to enforcing federal laws, adding "federal" after "to
enforce" in the first line would add clarity.

Part I, Background. The draft report addresses, in bullets, five concerns of installation
commanders. The first bullet uses the term "deputized" but the other four bullets do not. It
appears that all should. In addition, the first four concerns indicate uncertainty with existing
installation law enforcement authority. The Military Departments should be able to quite easily
address each of those concerns. Presently, the draft report does not further address these
concerns. The draft report might be amended to note that these four concerns indicate that there
may be uncertainty at DoD installations regarding the authority, scope and extent of existing
installation law enforcement authority. The draft report might also include a related
recommendation that the Military Departments consider publishing detailed guidelines in this
area that, at a minimum, address these concerns.

Background, Civilian Deputation of Military Law Enforcement Officials. The first sentence of this section might be expanded to add, "unless expressly authorized by the Constitution or an act of Congress." This addition would more accurately reflect the scope of the Posse Comitatus Act. The language in footnote 6 might be amended to begin, "The Act's proscriptions are ...." As written, the footnote could be read to mean that an Executive Branch agency may, by regulation, amend the applicability of a statute (in this case by making the statute applicable to Navy and Marine Corps personnel that the statute, by its terms, clearly does not include). The proposed language would help clarify that as a matter of policy the Department of Defense has applied the proscriptions present in the Act to Navy and Marine personnel, not the Act itself.

Part II, Evaluation Results and Recommendations, Need for DoD Policy and Process. One of the great risks we run in using deputation is that its use will exceed its legally authorized bounds. This section might better capture this key concern by adding "beyond their legal authority" after "their enforcement powers" in its last sentence.

Part II, Introduction. As addressed previously, this section might better consist solely of the last two paragraphs of the current "Introduction" section.

Part II, new section "Statutory and Regulatory Constraints?" As discussed previously, this new section would include what are presently the first six paragraphs of the "Introduction" section. This new section might best begin, however, by addressing and highlighting the legal authority for deputation and the resulting constraints. I submit possible language below. As proposed, the section would set the stage for, and lead directly into, the remaining sections. Proposed language:

"To determine the propriety of using deputized authority in view of statutory and regulatory constraints, we initially researched the legal authority for deputation. We found that no law or regulation expressly authorizes or prohibits deputation; the legal authority for deputation lies in the inherent authority of commanders to provide for the safety and security of their installations. This legal authority places significant constraints on the functions of authorizing and exercising deputation.

Constraints on Authorizing Deputation. The decision to obtain deputation authority from state or local civilian authorities must be made personally by the installation commander. The commander's decision must be based upon the commander's determination that obtaining deputation authority is necessary to ensure the safety and security of the installation or to accomplish some other military purpose inherent in the commander's mission. This determination must be based upon a comprehensive review of the particular facts at that installation, including those factors addressed in the following four sections of this report, and must be a reasonable and rational exercise of the commander's discretion.

Constraints on Executing Deputation Authority. Installation law enforcement personnel receive deputation authority solely to accomplish the law enforcement function for that installation as defined by the installation commander. They may therefore use their deputation authority only in furtherance of that defined law enforcement function. This constraint should be

2

a significant issue when discussing the acquisition of deputation authority with state and local authorities. State and local authorities must understand the limits the installation commander places on exercising the deputation authority. They must also accept that, if there is any conflict between a state or local requirement for exercising deputation and the installation commander's law enforcement requirements, installation law enforcement personnel must always comply with their commander's requirements. Any exercise of deputation authority beyond the limit set by the installation commander may subject installation law enforcement personnel to personal liability and may violate the Posse Comitatus Act (see below for additional information regarding this Act)."

What is now the first six paragraphs of the "Introduction" section would then follow beginning with, "We were unable to identify DoD policy...."

Recommendations. See my comment regarding DoD installation commanders' concerns in the paragraph titled "Part I, Background" above.

Appendix C, paragraph 1a. Adding "command law enforcement" before "function" might add clarity.

Appendix C, paragraph 2b. Although the decision-making authority should determine what must be included in the written justification, the draft report clearly indicates that certain information is essential. An additional sentence at the end of the paragraph suggesting information that should be included in the written justification may be helpful. A possible sentence is:

"The written justification should provide all relevant information including: (1) a detailed discussion of the issues identified in paragraphs 1a-d above, (2) the concurrence or non-concurrence, and any comments, of the appropriate United States Attorney who would handle legal actions arising from the exercise of the deputation authority, and (3) a written statement from the state or local official issuing the deputation authorization agreeing with the scope of the delegation authority as defined by the installation commander and acknowledging that deputized installation law enforcement personnel will not comply with any state or local requirements that conflict in any way with federal law or the installation commander's requirements."

Please call me if you have any questions regarding these comments.

James R. Schwenk
Associate Deputy General Counsel

3

Evaluation Team Members

Deputy Assistant Inspector General for Criminal Investigative Policy and Oversight, Office of the Assistant Inspector General for Investigations, Office of the Inspector General, Department of Defense.

John J. Perryman, Project Manager

Dennis J. Cullen, Investigative Review Specialist

Love A. Silverthorn, Investigative Review Specialist

www.ingramcontent.com/pod-product-compliance
Lightning Source LLC
Chambersburg PA
CBHW080632290526

45790CB00007B/3037